GOD'S DIVINE PLAN

for Healing and Health

How to Receive Healing for Your Body, Mind, and Soul

DR. GERARD KHOURIE

ISBN 979-8-88540-210-1 (paperback)
ISBN 979-8-88540-211-8 (digital)

Christian Faith Publishing
832 Park Avenue
Meadville, PA 16335
www.christianfaithpublishing.com

All scripture is taken from King James unless stated otherwise.
Ghostwritten and Edited by Laura Stamps.

Printed in the United States of America

Contents

Did you know the Bible contains the answer to every question you might have on any subject? It's true. And that includes the subject of *healing*.

Does God promise healing in His covenant?

Yes, He does!

If you're a born-again Christian, can you claim every healing promise in that covenant?

Yes, you can!

If you have questions about healing and how God plans to heal you, you've come to the right place. This book was written to answer those questions. Each chapter features a question about healing, the answer to that question, and scripture to back it up.

God has already provided healing for every physical, mental, and emotional disease, ailment, and illness known to man. The Bible is full of healing promises. All you have to do is claim those promises and receive your healing.

Don't know how to do that?

Not a problem!

I'll show you how to stand in your God-given authority to claim healing for yourself, your family, and your friends.

If you're sick and tired of being sick and tired, if you're ready to walk in God's perfect health, keep reading. This book was written for YOU!

Do sickness and disease come from God?

Answer

No! Everything good comes from God. Nothing else. In order for you to trust the Word of God for your healing, you must believe this. It's an elemental Biblical truth. You won't be able to benefit from this teaching until you believe everything good comes from God.

Okay, if nothing bad comes from God, then where does it come from? The devil. Sickness, disease, illness, everything negative, painful, and bad on earth comes from Satan.

Did you know healing is your divine right? It's true. In Luke 13, Jesus heals a woman who had been painfully disabled for eighteen years. What did Jesus say? He informed her and the crowd of onlookers that, because she was a daughter of Abraham, she had the right to be healed. In **Luke 13:16 (NKJ)**, "So ought not this woman, being a daughter of Abraham, whom Satan has bound—think of it—for eighteen years, be loosed from this bond on the Sabbath?".

What did He mean by that? He was referring to the covenant that belongs to all the children of Abraham. If you're a born-again Christian, you're also a child of Abraham. And every promise in this covenant belongs to you too.

How is this possible? When you were born again, you became a partner in this covenant, and Abraham became the father of your faith. **Romans 4:16 (NKJ)** states:

> Therefore *it is* of faith that *it might be* according to grace, so that the promise might be sure to all the seed, not only to those who are of the law, but also to those who are of the faith of Abraham, who is the father of us all.

That makes you a son or daughter of Abraham. And as a covenant son or daughter, you have the right to be healed.

God's only desire is to bless His covenant children. He will never plague you with problems and disasters. He will never use sickness and disease to "teach you something." That's not biblical. The Scripture tells us God teaches us through the Word (the Bible) and the Holy Spirit. Never through sickness and disease. **James 1:17** states, "Every good gift and every perfect gift is from above, and comes down from The Father of lights, with Whom there is no variation or shadow of turning."

God only always does good. And He doesn't change. Do you see it?

Would you call sickness good? No!

Is poverty good? No!

How about disasters? No!

Or premature death? No!

So if these things are not good, and God only does good, is it from God?

No! A thousand times no!

Now on the other hand, is healing good? Yes!

Is prosperity good? Yes!

How about protection for you and your loved ones? Oh yes!

A long fulfilled life? Yes!

These are the things we attribute to our heavenly father and not disaster. God always, only does good and there is no changing that!

How God anointed Jesus of Nazareth with The Holy Ghost and with power: Who went about doing good and healing all that were oppressed of the devil; for God was with Him.

—Acts 10:38

If sickness and disease don't come from God, where do they come from?

Answer

As I mentioned earlier, sickness and disease never come from God. Never. The Bible is crystal clear about that. The devil is the thief. The devil is the destroyer. He's the one who wants to steal your health and well-being. Not God. **John 10:10** states, "The thief does not come except to steal, and to kill, and to destroy. I have come that they may have life, and that they may have *it* more abundantly."

As a born-again Christian, you have become a child of the Most High God through the Blood of Jesus. That means you now have a covenant relationship with God, and every promise in that covenant belongs to you, including the promise of healing from every disease and ailment known to man.

God's desire is for the lives of His children to be filled with everything good in life: health, happiness, peace of mind, prosperity, joy, and so forth. **Acts 10:38** states, "How God anointed Jesus of Nazareth with The Holy Spirit and with power, Who went about doing good and healing all who were oppressed by the devil, for God was with Him."

The desire of the devil is for the lives of God's children to be filled with destruction. He is the author of everything that burdens you and makes your life miserable. He is the one who oppresses and harasses you, the one who torments you and makes you feel worthless and unloved.

Fortunately, you don't have to allow the devil to torment you. Once you become knowledgeable about your covenant rights, the devil will never gain a foothold in your life again.

Colossians 1:12–14 states:

> Giving thanks to The Father Who has qualified us to be partakers of the inheritance of the saints in the light. He has delivered us from the power of darkness and conveyed *us* into the kingdom of The Son of His love, in Whom we have redemption through His Blood, the forgiveness of sin

However, if through inaccurate teaching you believe God is the one who burdens you, makes you sick, or refuses to heal you, you won't exercise your covenant rights. You won't claim your healing. And that's exactly what the devil wants you to do.

If I am a born-again Christian, a child of The Most High God, why do I still struggle with sickness and disease?

Answer

You struggle with sickness and disease for the same reason many Christians do. You don't know your covenant rights. You don't realize you were delivered from the power of the devil over two thousand years ago. **Hosea 4:6** states, "My people are destroyed for lack of knowledge."

The Blood of Jesus is Holy Blood. The Blood that Jesus shed during His scourging and crucifixion was The *Blood Sacrifice* God needed in order to make you a child of His and a full partner in His covenant of blessing. The blood of animals could not accomplish this. God needed holy, sinless Blood. He needed The Blood of Jesus.

Your struggle with sickness and disease is simply a lack of knowledge. You are unaware of your covenant rights and what Jesus bought for you through His Blood.

As long as the devil can keep this understanding from you, he is free to torment you however he chooses. It's the only advantage he has. Your knowledge of your covenant with God destroys that advantage.

Now you can see why he works so hard to keep that knowledge from you and to flood your mind with doubt and inaccurate teaching. The last thing the devil wants is for you to become aware of your covenant rights because you'll realize you can claim your right to be healed.

Matthew 22:29 states, "Jesus answered and said to them, You are [a deceived] mistaken, not knowing The Scriptures nor the power of God."

Voice states, "You know neither God's Scriptures nor God's power—and so your assumptions are all wrong."

On that day, the devil will lose control of your health forever. Hallelujah!

What do I need in order to know the power of God?

Answer

All you'll ever need is knowledge of your covenant with God. It's only through this knowledge that you can know the power of God. It's only through this knowledge that you can put the power of God to work in your life. It's only through this knowledge that you'll be able to claim your healing. It's only through this knowledge that you can be healed. And it's only through this knowledge that you can walk in divine health for the rest of your life.

It's time to stop wishing you were healed. It's time to stop blaming God for your illness. As a born-again child of The Most High God, you're not powerless, and your situation is not hopeless.

All the knowledge you'll ever need is in God's Word. Think about it. When you became a born-again child of God, you received your eternal salvation. And that salvation came through your understanding of The Word. **Romans 1:16** states, "For I am not ashamed of the gospel of Christ, for It is the power of God to salvation for everyone who believes, for the Jew first and also for the Greek."

Salvation is a covenant relationship with God. What does that mean? It means you are now a born-again child of The Most High God. You're in covenant with God for all eternity. And that means all the promises in that covenant belong to you.

Salvation, as well as all these promises, came to you through The Word. That's how much power The Word of God contains. The Gospel of Christ is the power of God. All you need to receive your healing is knowledge of what The Word contains. Mix that with faith in The Word, and you've got all the power you'll ever need to receive your healing and walk in divine health for the rest of your life. **Romans 4:16 (Passion)** states:

> The promise depends on faith so that it can be experienced as a grace-gift, and now it extends to all the descendants of Abraham. This promise is not only meant for those who obey the law, but also to those who enter into the faith of Abraham, the father of us all.

The Word operates through faith. Faith in God's Word is essential. No faith, no power. In chapter 4 of Romans, we learn that Abraham walked in faith, and God called this *righteousness*. As a born-again child of God, you're the righteousness of God. And you're called to walk in faith too. **Romans 4:19–22** states:

> And not being weak in faith, he did not consider his own body, already dead [since he was about a hundred years old], and the deadness of Sarah's womb. He did not waver at the promise of God through unbelief, but was strengthened in faith, giving glory to God, and being fully convinced that what He had promised He was also able to perform. And therefore "it was accounted to him for righteousness."

The world walks in a different direction. It always has. It walks in fear. And fear is a demonic spirit. Every day we're bombarded by fearful health warnings, ads for hundreds of medications, and frightening news of the latest disease or virus. It takes tremendous effort to avoid this negativity when it's everywhere.

Don't listen to it. If you listen to it, you'll consider it. Refuse to listen to it and refuse to consider it. That's what I do. I know my covenant rights. I don't need to hear the latest medical warnings. That's a waste of my time. I'd much rather spend my time considering what

God has to say about health and healing. Meditating on my covenant promises is all the *considering* I need to do! **Psalm 1:2–3** states:

> But his delight in the law of The Lord;
> and in His law doth he meditate day and night.
> And he shall be like a tree planted by the rivers of
> water, that bringeth forth his fruit in his season;
> his leaf also shall not wither; and whatsoever he
> doeth shall prosper.

If the Word of God is all the power I'll ever need, then how do I put that power into practice?

Answer

The Word of God is not only powerful, but it's also supernatural. Why? Because The Word of God came to earth in the form of a man, Jesus Christ. And Jesus is all-powerful. That's why Christians often say The Word speaks to them. It does. When you hold The Bible, you're holding Jesus in your hands. Now that's POWER!

Therefore, The Bible is not a collection of fables or myths or stories. The Bible is the sheath that contains the most powerful sword in this world: The Word of God. When you read this supernatural Word, and it saturates your heart and mind, it creates faith. And that faith is the power in your sword.

Use that sword to attack whatever sickness or disease the devil is trying to put on your mind, body, or emotions. Attack it by confessing The Word in faith. Claim those healing Scriptures in faith. Keep attacking with The Word until you receive your victory. Persistence is the key!

Hebrews 4:12 states:

> For The Word of God *is* living and powerful, and sharper than any two-edged sword, piercing even to the division of soul and spirit, and of joints and marrow, and is a discerner of the thoughts and intents of the heart.

Passion states:

> For we have the Living Word of God, which is full of energy, like a two-mouthed sword. It will even penetrate to the very core of our being where soul and spirit, bone and marrow meet! It interprets and reveals the true thoughts and secret motives of our hearts.

How is faith for healing connected to faith for the forgiveness of my sins?

Answer

Psalm 103:1–3 states:

> Bless The Lord, O my soul; And all that is
> within me, *bless* His Holy Name!
> Bless The Lord, O my soul, And forget not
> all His benefits:
> Who forgives all your iniquities, Who heals
> all your diseases.

In Psalm 103, The Word says God forgives all your sins. It also says He heals all your diseases.

This is a faith issue. Do you believe when you were born again, all your sins were forgiven? Yes, you do. Then you must also believe The God Who forgives all your sins is also The God Who heals all your diseases.

Forgiveness of sins is easy to believe, isn't it? But it's not so easy to believe God heals all your diseases. Not that He *will* heal all your diseases, or that He *can* heal all your diseases, but that He *has healed* all your diseases. Your healing (spirit, soul, and body) has already been accomplished. It happened the moment you were born again.

The problem is you never realized that because you didn't have enough knowledge of your covenant. And that knowledge can only come through meditating on The Word.

Think about it. If you believe the first part of that Scripture is true (He forgives all your sins), why can't you believe the second part is true as well (He heals all your diseases)?

Spend some time meditating on this Scripture. Consider what God is saying here. He heals all your diseases. Every sickness, every illness, every disease known to man. Same God, same Scripture, same Word, same Holy Spirit, same power.

There is power in spending time in The Word and meditating on the supernatural truths and promises it contains. If you hit a mental roadblock when you're studying The Word, just pray and ask The Holy Spirit to open your eyes and give you understanding.

Then keep going. Never stop meditating on the Scripture and your covenant promises. You no longer have to be sick and healed, sick and healed, sick and healed. Now you can use the power of your faith in The Word to not only be healed but also to remain healed forever.

Psalm 1:2–3 states:

> But his delight *is* in the law of the Lord,
> And in His law he meditates day and night.
> He shall be like a tree Planted by the rivers
> of water, That brings forth its fruit in its season,
> Whose leaf also shall not wither; And whatever
> he does shall prosper.

Since sickness and disease come from the curse, is there still a curse on the earth?

Answer

Yes. Sin entered the earth when Adam and Eve chose to believe the serpent (Satan) instead of God. And that curse remains today.

Most Christians think God gave the Jewish people the first set of laws with Moses. But the first set of laws were those God used to create the earth and to protect it from being cursed by Satan. If those laws were broken, the curse would come on the earth.

And that's exactly what happened when Adam and Eve broke those laws in the Garden of Eden. Their disobedience allowed the earth to be cursed.

Genesis 3:17 states:

> Then to Adam He said, "Because you have heeded the voice of your wife, and have eaten from the tree of which I commanded you, saying, 'You shall not eat of it': "Cursed *is* the ground for your sake; In toil you shall eat *of* it All the days of your life."

So yes, the curse is still in full operation on the earth. And yes, this curse is what causes all the things in life we don't want.

If I'm a born-again Christian, am I still cursed?

Answer

As a born-again child of The Most High God, you have been redeemed from the curse of the law. That is a fact, and it always will be. **Galatians 3:13 (Passion)** states:

> Yet, Christ paid the full price to set us free from the curse of the law. He absorbed the curse completely as He became a curse in our place. For it is written: "Everyone who is hung upon a tree is cursed."

Redemption is an incredible gift. We could never have redeemed ourselves. Only Jesus could do that for us. In addition to the Ten Commandments God gave to Moses, there are over six hundred additional commandments. No human could possibly satisfy all those laws, which is why the Jewish nation ritually slaughtered a lamb every year as a blood sacrifice for the redemption of their sins.

But animal sacrifices were just a temporary fix. It was redemption with a time limit: one year. Something permanent had to be done. And that was the gift Jesus gave to us. He became the perfect sacrifice for us through His precious, sinless Blood, a sacrifice that had to be offered only once in order to redeem us from the curse forever.

In **2 Corinthians 5:21**, it states, "For He made Him Who knew no sin *to be* sin for us, that we might become the righteousness of God in Him."

Passion states, "For God made The Only One who did not know sin to become sin for us, so that we might become the righteousness of God through our union with Him."

If, as a born-again child of God, I'm free from the curse, can it still torment me?

Answer

Yes, even though you've been redeemed from the curse, it can still torment you and control every aspect of your life.

How is this possible? It's a consequence of a lack of knowledge of your covenant and how it operates. For example, if you don't know healing belongs to you as one of your covenant rights, you'll speak sickness and disease. Likewise, if you don't know the laws of your covenant that govern divine healing, you won't receive your healing, and you certainly won't be able to walk in divine health 24-7.

The minute you feel a drip in the back of your throat, you'll begin agreeing with sickness and disease (the curse) and speaking it into manifestation. You'll tell everyone you meet you're "coming down with a cold." Likewise, when you feel an ache or a pain, you'll tell everyone your back is out, or you have arthritis.

Deuteronomy 30:19 states:

> I call heaven and earth as witnesses today
> against you, *that* I have set before you life and
> death, blessing and cursing; therefore choose life,
> that both you and your descendants may live.

When you agree with the curse, you give it *permission* to control that area of your life.

As a born-again child of God, you've already been healed of every disease or illness known to man, which is every disease and illness controlled by the curse. Healing is part of your covenant.

But the power of that covenant is in your words. When you speak illness, you give Satan permission to make you sick with whatever ailment you're speaking.

Isaiah 53:5 states, "But He *was* wounded for our transgressions, *He was* bruised for our iniquities; The chastisement for our peace *was* upon Him, And by His stripes we are healed."

That's why so many born-again Christians are sick or dying. They don't know how their covenant works. They don't realize they give the curse control of any situation in their lives simply by agreeing with it mentally (meditating on it), emotionally (giving in to fear), or vocally (speaking illness).

The choice is yours, and that choice is in your mouth. As a covenant child of The Most High God, your responsibility is to agree with the promises in your covenant mentally, emotionally, and vocally. Never agree with the curse.

Only by speaking your covenant healing will you receive your healing. Start today. Choose life by speaking what you desire. Speak healing!

But the reality is I'm sick! That's a fact. Why can't I speak the facts?

Answer

Sickness and disease are only realities for those who are not born again and not in a covenant relationship with God.

But you are. You're a child of The Most High God. Sickness and disease are NOT your reality. They are NOT your *facts* because they're not true of you. Your truth is what your covenant says about you. And it says you're healed. That's the only fact you need to be concerned with.

In **1 Peter 2:24 (Voice)**, it states:

> He took on our sins in His body *when He*
> *died* on the cross so that we, being dead to sin,
> can live for righteousness. *As The Scripture says,*
> "Through His wounds, you were healed."

Now I'm not saying it's easy to speak healing when you feel lousy. It's not. It's hard. But war is hard. Most Christians don't understand we're in a constant battle with Satan. Speaking your covenant, which is the Word of God, is the supernatural weapon you've been given to win this battle every time. It's more powerful than anything Satan could ever use against you.

However, the key to winning this battle is persistence and consistency. Persist by continuing to speak your healing no matter how bad you feel. Remain consistent by speaking your healing every day, all day, day after day until the symptoms of illness disappear, and your healing manifests. Be persistent and consistent. That's the only way to win the battle against Satan.

There's a good example of this in the Old Testament (Numbers 13 and 14). God sent twelve spies into the Promised Land. A few of those spies returned and spoke victory according to God's Word. The rest returned and spoke what they perceived to be the *facts* of the situation. God blessed the few who spoke His Word. But He called the fact-reporting of the others an *evil report*. And they were cursed for it.

The 12 men Moses sent to explore Canaan (the promised land) came back and reported that yes, the place is wonderful, but we can't take on the giants and the armies. There's big this and big that. And the truth is, there were giants and there were armies. There were all those things the men reported, and the walls were high. But, when they told what they saw, God said they gave an evil report. (Numbers 13:32 and 14:37)

Why would God call the facts they reported, an evil report? I mean, after all it was true in the natural. They said what they saw. What the facts were, and yet God called it an evil report.

Well God had said to the Israelites, *I have given you the land (past tense), go in and possess it.* (Deuteronomy 1:8 NIV)

It wasn't that they had lied. It's that they reported the negatives.

They reported the facts. Even though God said I have given you the land, they said, "We can't take it! We can't win against those giants!" They contradicted God.

The facts were, there were giants in the land. There were great armies with chariots in the land. There were high walled cities in the land, but God had said, I have given you the land, go in and possess it.

They believed what they saw over what God said. Over The Word of God, and God called that an evil report. And because of that, that generation died in the wilderness and never got into Canaan's land and therefore never received the promise.

Now to your situation. God said you are healed (Isaiah 53:5 + 1st Peter 2:24). So when you say you're sick, or I've got Cancer, could you be giving an evil report?

God said, "I became poor so you can be rich." (2 Corinthians 8:9) So when you say "I'm broke!" Could that be an evil report? God said, "You can do all things through Christ who strengthens you."

(Philippians 4:13) If you say, "I can't do it, I'm not able!" Might that be an evil report?

I know the facts are present, but The Word of God is bigger and stronger then any facts you might see. If you stand on The Word of God, the facts will line up with The Word.

Now you can go right back and operate under the curse. Go around saying *I'm sick* long enough and see what happens

So, yes, there's still a curse on the earth, but we are redeemed from the curse. However, we can go back and forth between the curse and the blessings as much as we want. Our choice, our decision. (Deuteronomy 30:19)

The facts in your situation may seem grim. But The Word of God (the promises in your covenant) is more powerful than any fact. Continue to believe and speak The Word of your covenant. Persist in speaking it and remain consistent in speaking it.

Philippians 4:13 states, "I can do all things through Christ Who strengthens me."

Eventually, those troublesome *facts* will begin to agree with what you've been speaking! Even while going to the doctor or taking the medication, keep proclaiming in faith The Word of God. Faith will often defy logic!

Are there other ways I can be tormented by the curse?

Answer

Yes, even though you have been redeemed from the curse, you can still operate under the curse. Let me elaborate.

I am from South Africa, so let's pretend South Africa is the curse and America is the blessing (I said pretend. South Africa is not the curse. This is just for illustration purposes), and I get on a plane and move from South Africa to America—from the curse to the blessing. Remember, The Bible says Christ has redeemed you *from* the curse. That means if I'm from somewhere, I'm not there now. So, if I move to America, I'm no longer in South Africa under the curse. But, do you know, I can buy a ticket and go right back to the curse? I can go back to South Africa tomorrow.

That's what Christians are doing. They are buying tickets back to the curse. How do you buy a ticket? When you say, *I'm sick!* You just bought a ticket back to the curse. *I'm broke!* And you just bought a ticket back to the curse. *I can't understand it!* You just bought a ticket back to the curse. *I can't do it!* You're buying tickets left, right, and center. Some are even flying first class. And it's costing.

You put yourself back under the curse when you *agree* with the curse. When you say *I am sick*, you put yourself back under the curse. Christ said *that by the stripes on My back you are healed (Isaiah 53:5)*. The blessing is *I'm healed*. The curse is *I am sick*.

Negative thoughts are also dangerous saboteurs, placing you under the dominion of the curse. Negative thoughts lead to negative words and actions. Godly thoughts lead to godly words and actions. Do you indulge in negative thoughts? If so, repent and vow to think only godly thoughts. The only thoughts a born-again child of The Most High God should be thinking are those thoughts that agree with The Word of God.

Fear will place every aspect of your life under the authority of the curse. Fear is the opposite of faith. Yet they both operate according to the same principle. Both fear and faith believe in something that can't be seen. Fear is the practice of believing something negative will happen. Faith is the practice of believing something that already happened two thousand-plus years ago. Choose faith!

Acts 4:29 states, "Now, Lord, look on their threats, and grant to Your servants that with all boldness they may speak Your word."

In **2 Timothy 1:7**, it states, "For God hath not given us the spirit of fear; but of power, and of love, and of a sound mind."

Lack of knowledge definitely keeps you under the dominion of the curse. Too many Christians operate in the realm of ignorance. They just don't know The Word. They haven't taken the time to read The Bible every day, study The Bible, meditate on The Scriptures they've read, and gain adequate knowledge of The Bible.

You can hear this lack of knowledge in their prayers. If you know The Word, you're certain of God's will for you. If you're uncertain of God's will, you suffer from a lack of knowledge. Any time you hear a Christian pray, "If it is Your will," you can be sure that Christian is suffering from a lack of knowledge.

In **1 John 5:14–15**, it states:

> Now this is the confidence that we have in Him, that if we ask anything according to His will, He hears us. And if we know that He hears us, whatever we ask, we know that we have the petitions that we have asked of Him.

The Word of God is the Will of God! (A person's last will and testament)

This is especially true of healing prayers. There is no *if* in matters of healing.

Hosea 4:6 (AMP) states, "My people are destroyed for lack of knowledge [of My law, where I reveal My will]."

It is God's desire for every born-again child of His to be healed. There is no *maybe* to healing. As far as God is concerned, there is only *yes*. Yes, healing is now. Yes, healing is for you. Yes, you are already healed. All you have to do is claim it.

The Bible is God's will in black-and-white. Know The Word of God. Think The Word of God. Speak The Word of God. Act on The Word of God. Make The Word of God your 24/7 lifestyle. That's how you remain in the blessing. That's how you receive your healing.

As a born-again Christian, should I go to the doctor or use medication?

Answer

Yes. If you think you should go to the doctor, that's a sign that you should go. Same with medication. If you think you should take medication, take it.

God heals us. That's a fact. He has promised that in His Word and in His covenant. But we must have enough faith to receive that healing. It takes time to build your faith to that level. It takes time to increase your knowledge of your covenant. Only you know your level of faith at any given moment. Only you know if you have enough faith to receive your healing.

In the beginning, you won't have that level of faith. That's normal. You're in the faith-building stage. Don't deny yourself access to doctors and medication when you need it. Continue to build your faith and increase your knowledge of God's Word during those times. Don't allow it to derail you.

Doctors are a resource God uses when necessary to bring healing to His people. God and doctors have the same goal. They both want you healed and well.

Think about it. God has given us a planet stocked with healing plants, herbs, and seeds. It's no wonder many of our modern medications are derived from nature. God has given scientists the knowledge to extract these plants from the earth and to manufacture medicines from them. God has given medical researchers the ability to discover the healing qualities of these plants and to use them to create cures for a host of ailments and diseases.

Genesis 1:29 (NIV) states, "Then God said, 'I give you every seed-bearing plant on the face of the whole earth and every tree that has fruit with seed in it. They will be yours for food.'"

You're the only one who knows if you have enough faith to be healed at this stage in your life. If you feel your faith is strong enough, and you have complete peace in your heart about it, then trust The Word for your healing.

But if you know your faith isn't to that level, and you don't have peace in your heart, go to the doctor. The choice is yours and yours alone. Do what you feel you need to do. It's that simple.

What is it like to live day by day at a high faith level?

Answer

Every day in every situation, I do my best to trust God, His Word, and my covenant. I haven't been to a doctor in years. God is The source of all healing for me. My faith is strong, and I have peace in my heart.

Romans 4:19 states, "And not being weak in faith, he did not consider his own body, already dead [since he was about a hundred years old], and the deadness of Sarah's womb."

Passion: "In spite of being nearly one hundred years old when the promise of having a son was made, his faith was so strong that it could not be undermined by the fact that he and Sarah were incapable of conceiving a child."

However, that doesn't mean I don't get symptoms of illness or aches and pains from time to time. I do. Does Satan still try to attack me with sickness and disease? Yes, he does.

But when those situations arise, and I experience troubling physical symptoms, I do what Abraham did: I don't even consider them. Like Abraham, I'm fully persuaded that God is able to perform what He has promised.

Romans 4:20–21 states:

> He staggered not at the promise of God through unbelief; but was strong in faith, giving glory to God; And being fully persuaded that, what He had promised, He was able also to perform.

When I say I don't consider any symptom of sickness and disease, what I mean is I don't think about it. I don't meditate on it. I don't worry about it. I don't talk about it. I don't tell anyone. Not even my wife or children.

Psalm 1:2 states, "But his delight *is* in the law of The Lord, And in His law he meditates day and night."

Speaking about sickness and disease gives it power. Words and thoughts about physical symptoms feed those symptoms until they bloom into a full-blown illness. My goal is to deny Satan that pleasure. I have no intention of using my valuable energy to feed the works of the devil and the power of the curse. My goal is to take all fearful thoughts captive by remaining in agreement with The Word.

Job 3:25 states, "For the thing I greatly feared has come upon me, And what I dreaded has happened to me."

When you're fully persuaded that you are healed according to The Word of God which is a promise of God, you'll walk in divine health all the days of your life. You won't need doctors to heal you. You have The Great Healer, and He's all you need. He is your SOURCE. Period.

Bonus scripture

In **2 Corinthians 10:3 (Passion)**, it states:

> For although we live in the natural realm, we don't wage a military campaign employing human weapons, *using manipulation to achieve our aims.* Instead, our *spiritual* weapons are energized with divine power to effectively dismantle the defenses *behind which people hide.* We can demolish every deceptive fantasy that opposes God and break through every arrogant attitude that is raised up in defiance of the true knowledge of God. We capture, like prisoners of war, every thought and insist that it bow in obedience to The Anointed One.

How will I know when I've reached a "fully persuaded" level of faith?

Answer

The answer is simple. If you have to ask this question, you're not there yet. Uncertainty about your faith is a sure sign you haven't reached the 100 percent faith level. In that case, don't take a chance. See a doctor.

How do I know this? Because when you're fully persuaded, you have peace in your heart. There's no need to wonder about your faith. You know you've already received your healing according to your covenant. Now you're just waiting for your healing to manifest.

And you have no doubt that it will.

Romans 8:25 (Passion) states, "So because our hope is set on what is yet to be seen, we patiently keep on waiting for its fulfillment."

When I reached a strong faith level, I realized I no longer needed to know about the inner workings of my body. I don't even need to know where all my organs are located. Why? Because Satan could use that knowledge to tempt me the next time he attacks with a physical symptom. Immediately, my mind would try to locate the organ that corresponds with the symptom in that area of my body. From there, it's just a downward spiral into worry and fear. No thanks!

Romans 8:5 states, "For those who live according to the flesh set their minds on the things of the flesh, but those *who live* according to The Spirit, the things of The Spirit."

Our words and thoughts are powerful. They're containers of creative energy. What you think about, meditate on, worry about, obsess over creates more of the same. Words and thoughts about sickness and disease create more sickness and disease. They feed the works of the curse.

I'd much rather follow the example of my spiritual father, Abraham, and not even consider my own body. With The Great Healer as my SOURCE, I trust every organ, wherever it may be located, is healthy and working well. And if that's good enough for Abraham, that's good enough for me!

Philippians 4:8 states:

> Finally, brethren, whatsoever things are true, whatsoever things are honest, whatsoever things are just, whatsoever things are pure, whatsoever things are lovely, whatsoever things are of good report; if there be any virtue, and if there be any praise, think on these things.

What should my faith walk look like?

Answer

It's a process. You study the Word every day by reading it and meditating on passages of the Scripture you'd like to memorize in order to plant them deep in your heart. You confess those memorized Scriptures every day, especially the healing Scriptures. You confess them when you feel fine. You confess them when Satan attacks your body with symptoms of sickness or disease.

Every day, your faith grows. Every day, you learn to trust The Great Healer a little more. During this growth period, you may have to take medication for an illness or symptom. That's okay. Just because you took two aspirin for a headache doesn't mean you're not walking in faith.

Pray as you take medication by saying, "Thank You, Jesus, that I'm healed according to 1 Peter 2:24. Thank You that I walk in divine health every day. By Your stripes, I am healed!"

In **1 Peter 2:24**, "Who Himself bore our sins in His Own Body on the tree, that we, having died to sins, might live for righteousness—by Whose stripes you were healed."

What are you doing? You're practicing. You're learning, growing, and developing your faith.

You take those aspirins in faith and keep moving forward. No need to advertise it. No need to open the door to Satan by telling everyone, especially someone who might derail your faith with their unbelief. Avoid anyone who might condemn you for taking aspirin. Avoid anyone who might try to make you feel guilty. Guard your faith, guard your mind, guard your speech

Romans 8:1 (Voice) states:

> Therefore, now no condemnation awaits those who are living in Jesus The Anointed, *The Liberating King,* because when you live in The Anointed One, Jesus, *a new law takes effect.* The law of The Spirit of life *breathes into you and* liberates you from the law of sin and death. God did something the law could never do. *You see, human flesh took its toll on God's law. In and of itself, the law is not weak; but* the flesh weakens it. So to condemn the sin that was *ruling* in the flesh, God sent His Own Son, bearing the likeness of sinful flesh, as a sin offering. Now we are able to live up to the justice demanded by the law. But that ability has not come from living by our fallen human nature; it has come because we walk according to the movement of The Spirit in our lives.

If you live your life animated by the flesh—*namely, your fallen, corrupt nature*—then your mind is focused on the matters of the flesh. But if you live your life animated by The Spirit—*namely, God's indwelling presence*—then your focus is on the work of The Spirit. A mind focused on the flesh is doomed to death, but a mind focused on The Spirit will find full life and complete peace.

If you've always suffered from allergies of any kind or a sensitive stomach, do what you have to do to maintain your health while you build your faith for divine healing.

One day, those ailments will completely disappear, and your healing will manifest. But until then, do what you need to do in order to maintain your health. And allow no one to condemn you for it.

But some people believe, and they die anyway. What about those who believe but are not healed?

Answer

John 15:5 states, "I Am the vine, you *are* the branches. He who abides in Me, and I in him, bears much fruit; for without Me you can do nothing."

You can't do anything without God. Fortunately, you don't have to. You're a born-again child of The Most High God. You're the temple of The Holy Spirit, which means The Holy Spirit dwells within you every minute of every day.

With God, you can overcome allergies, hepatitis, arthritis, cancer, and every ailment known to man. I'll say that again: You can overcome anything and everything the devil throws at you simply with The Word of God. And that's a biblical truth.

But you have to think correctly. You have to act correctly. Faith is not blind. Faith comes with knowledge.

Should Christians go to the doctor and use medication? Yes. If your children are sick, and your prayers don't appear to be working, go to the doctor. Go to the ER, the hospital, go wherever you feel you need to go to receive healing for yourself, your children, your family.

Don't feel guilty about it. And don't allow anyone to condemn you for it. Go to that doctor, take that medication, and pray, "Lord, I thank you for the faith growing inside me."

However, as your faith strengthens and your heart, mind, and soul are nourished with the Scripture every day, you'll get to the point where you realize you don't need to go to the doctor every time you're faced with a troubling physical symptom.

Joshua 1:8 (Voice) states:

> Let *the words from* the book of the law be always on your lips. Meditate on them day and night so that you may be careful to live by all that is written in it. If you do, as you make your way *through this world,* you will prosper and always find success.

But it takes time to reach this level of faith. And that was certainly true for me. But now, years later, I can honestly say I haven't been to the doctor in many years. I trust God. I trust The Great Healer. I've studied The Word, I've eaten The Word, I've slept on The Word, and I've lived The Word. The Word has become part of who I am.

And that's what it takes. When you're constantly in The Word, The Word becomes part of your life. It becomes part of your physical body. The healing Scriptures become part of who you are. When that happens, you'll walk in divine health every day as I do.

I've said all of this to illustrate what it takes to get to the 100 percent faith level. But here's the thing. You never know if someone is really at that level or not. That person may pray all the time, quote the right scriptures, and talk the talk, but no one really knows what's in that person's heart. Only God knows.

For example, I once knew a pastor with a church similar to ours who taught on healing. Many were healed in his church. He even laid hands on a man who was blind, and that man's eyes opened, and he could see. That pastor was on fire for God. He loved God.

Years later, he developed cancer. I visited him in the hospital and offered to pray for him. He told me he was standing strong in faith. He assured me that he had already been prayed for and didn't need more prayer.

He died three months later. I couldn't understand it. It didn't make sense. So I prayed about it. Why did he die? I had to know. Something must have happened. What was it?

I said to God, "Lord, I need to know why. I need to know what happened." And God allowed his sister to show me what had happened.

His sister who was his associate Pastor told me, "While I was at the hospital with him, he said to me, 'don't merge our church with such and such church. I don't want you to join our churches together.'"

Well, if you're in faith and you're going to be healed, why are you telling someone what to do if you're going to be here and you are still the senior Pastor? Could it be he was preparing just in case? Remember, faith is to be fully persuaded like our spiritual father, Abraham. There are no exceptions. There's no room for doubt. If someone is standing strong in faith and believes he or she has received healing according to The Word, there's no need to make plans "just in case."

And that's why he died. He was talking the talk, but he wasn't walking the walk. In other words, there was doubt mixed with this pastor's faith. But no one knew it. Only God knew.

Although I was saddened by this pastor's death, I never allowed it to affect my faith. Don't be moved by what happens to other Christians, or what others are going through. Only be moved by The Word of God.

Psalm 119:97 (Voice) states, "Oh, how I love Your law! I fix my mind on it all day long."

We all know great Christians who pray, quote scripture, and talk the talk. But we don't know if those people are walking in 100 percent faith. Only God knows.

In **1 Timothy 4:15**, it states, "Meditate on these things; give yourself entirely to them, that your progress may be evident to all."

How is righteousness connected to 100 percent faith for healing?

Answer

Years ago, I prayed for a fourteen-year-old boy in a healing line at our church. He had diabetes.

I prayed over him with the elders of the church, anointed him with oil, and laid hands on him, according to The Word of God.

James 5:14–15 states:

> Is anyone among you sick? Let him call for the elders of the church, and let them pray over him, anointing him with oil in The Name of The Lord. And the prayer of faith will save the sick, and The Lord will raise him up. And if he has committed sins, he will be forgiven.

After that healing service, he went home with his family. The first thing he did when he arrived was walking into the kitchen, open the refrigerator, and take out a big slice of chocolate strawberry cake.

Romans 4:20–22 states:

> He staggered not at the promise of God through unbelief; but was strong in faith, giving glory to God; And being fully persuaded that, what He had promised, He was able also to perform. And therefore it was imputed to him for righteousness.

His mother followed him into the kitchen, horrified at what he was about to do. Before he could eat the first bite, she reminded him that he was on a restricted diet. Diabetics can't eat cake. It's too dangerous.

But he wasn't worried. He reminded her that things had changed. He was healed. He had been prayed for according to The Word. He believed The Word. And as far as he was concerned, he was healed.

At that moment, his mother had a choice to make. She could stand in faith with her son and agree with The Word. Or she could operate in fear and disbelief, continue to argue with him, and eventually destroy his faith.

She chose faith and watched him finish the cake. He enjoyed every bite. And he never had another problem with food. He was completely healed of diabetes, just like he believed.

That's 100 percent faith. That's how you know you've reached that level in your faith journey. There was never a doubt in that boy's mind. He believed The Word. He believed God would do what He had promised. And that was that. Period.

James 2:23 states, "And The Scripture was fulfilled which saith, Abraham believed God, and it was imputed unto him for righteousness: and he was called the Friend of God."

When you're in 100 percent faith, you call yourself healed even when you don't feel like it. You don't tell anyone who will listen about your problems. As far as you're concerned, you've already received your healing, and you're just waiting for the physical manifestation of that healing. Sometimes, the physical manifestation is instant. Sometimes it takes a while. None of that matters to you. You received your healing when you prayed. You are healed. And that's all you need to know.

And that's exactly what your spiritual father, Abraham, did. He received his healing from God and never gave it another thought. He knew God was faithful to perform what He had promised, and that was good enough for him.

That's confidence in The Word. That's 100 percent faith. God calls that kind of faith *righteousness*. And God always rewards righteousness!

Psalm 58:11 states, "So that men will say, 'Surely *there is* a reward for the righteous; Surely He is God Who judges in the earth.'"

Psalm 37:39–40 states:

> But the salvation of the righteous *is* from The Lord; *He is* their strength in the time of trouble. And The Lord shall help them and deliver them; He shall deliver them from the wicked, And save them, Because they trust in Him.

Psalm 34:15, 17, and 19 state:

> The eyes of The Lord *are* on the righteous,
> And His ears *are open* to their cry.
> *The righteous* cry out, and The Lord hears,
> And delivers them out of all their troubles.
> Many *are* the afflictions of the righteous,
> But The Lord delivers him out of them all.

SUMMARY

1. *Does God cause us to become sick?*

No. It's God's will for us to be in health.

2. *Since sickness and disease come from the curse, is there still a curse on the earth?*

Yes, but Jesus Christ has redeemed us from the curse.

3. *As a child of God, can the curse still torment me and control every aspect of my life?*

Yes. But only if your thoughts and words agree with the curse. However, if your thoughts and words agree with what God says in His Word, you will be blessed by God.

4. *Should a born-again Christian go to a doctor and take medication?*

Until you know deep in your heart that you are healed, until you have no doubts, until you are fully persuaded you are healed, until you are operating in 100 percent faith, and until your doctor confirms you are healed, I would highly recommend and suggest you go to the doctor and take the medications prescribed.

If you have never accepted the free gift of salvation and believe in Jesus, please confess the following Prayer:

> Dear Heavenly Father, I come to You today, acknowledging my need for salvation.
>
> I confess my sins and ask for Your forgiveness. Create in me a brand new spirit.
>
> I believe Jesus Christ lived and died that I might live. He took my sin, punishment, judgement and sickness on Himself so that I don't have to. On the third day He rose from the dead.
>
> According to **John 3:3-5** and **Romans 10:9-10** …if you confess with your mouth The Lord Jesus and believe in your heart that God has raised Him from the dead, you will be saved. **10** For with the heart one believes unto righteousness, and with the mouth confession is made unto salvation.
>
> I have done this today and according to Your Word, heaven is now my home. God is now my Father.
>
> My name is in the book of life. I am now born again., I am a child of God.
>
> Thank You Lord for Your love and the free gift of eternal life. In Jesus' Name, I pray. Amen.

If you meant that prayer you are now a child of God. Find a good Bible based church to attend.

Blessings on your new found life!

www.ingramcontent.com/pod-product-compliance
Lightning Source LLC
Chambersburg PA
CBHW031003180726
47993CB00018B/1533